Lessons Learned in Manufacturing Management

2019 by Terry W. Offerle

Some Foundational Background

In the late 1980's, a manufacturing plant in rural Ohio was struggling. It had been a very profitable operation for many years, and still was profitable, less so year over year for the prior 10 years. In the 70's, it was seen as the "Flagship" of the Corporation. But as costs increased and profits declined, management was unable to find a way to improve operationally and offset inflation. They resorted to putting a stop to spending in order to try to maintain the earnings that were expected by the Corporation. This resulted in a downward performance spiral that was destined to get worse month over month. Management knew that the decisions they were making to stop spending, postpone needed maintenance activities, buy supplies in smaller quantities, use cheaper raw materials and supplies, etc., would eventually come back to haunt them. However, they felt they had no choice. If they didn't report better earnings results, they would lose their jobs.

Eventually, they lost their jobs anyway. In the fall of 1990, a new Plant Manager was hired for the plant. He very quickly went to work and started to change the way the plant was managed, how they manufactured, their old policies and practices, and pretty much everything they did. The results were almost immediate, and substantial. For the next two and a half years, the plant was on a course of continual improvement that was greater than anyone's expectations.

The new plant manager wanted to write a book about his first two years in this plant. He wanted to call it "The Return of the Flagship". He would work on it from time to time, and would bring in pages that he wrote and have some of us – his staff – read them and give him feedback. Of course, they were perfectly written. (They weren't, but no one was going to tell the boss that!)

Eventually, he moved on to another job, and then another company, and the book was never written. It's too bad, because it would have been very interesting reading. The plant had made a miraculous recovery from the point when he started. He left behind a management team that were now disciples in the ways of what we at that time called JIT Manufacturing. Over the next few years, that group of young men took what they had learned and put it to very good use. Many of them became Plant Managers, and all of them eventually moved on to bigger and better opportunities. As of today, that group includes 1 CEO, 2 SVP of Operations, 2 Global Operations Managers, 2 retired operational executives, and (my personal choice for the best job of all) 1 Host at Disney (and former plant manager).

Unfortunately, as these people began to leave the plant in Ohio, it slowly began to retreat to its old ways. Inventory grew, labor was not managed very well, productivity started to slide, then nose dive. Leadership had again changed, and so did their priorities and methods. In the 25 or so years since then, the plant has been up and down, depending on management and their "flavor of the day" style of management. There were months that were stellar, and there were months that we'd barely break even. The one thing that was consistent was that we were very inconsistent.

As of my retirement in 2016, the plant was back on top, leading their group of plants in Quality, Cost Management, Delivery, and Earnings. The plant made up less than 20% of the entire Group sales dollars, but also made up more than 65% of the group's profit.

I had worked for the subject company for more than 43 years. I held a variety of positions in the Company, from starting in the Engineering field to Global Director of Lean Manufacturing with many, many stops in the middle. I worked at the subject plant during the bad times, the good times, the bad times, and back to the good times again. The fact of the matter is that I have learned an amazing amount about operational excellence, and about operational ignorance. I truly believe that I learned at least as much, if not more, by working in bad organizations with poor managers, as I did with great organizations and great leaders and managers.

The reason I wanted to write this small book is to take the experiences I have had, both good and bad, and try to relate them in a way that will help you become a better informed manager, and recognize the signals that should trigger you to become the best at what you do every day. I also hope to allow you to see why a plant that is the "Flagship" can deteriorate, possibly some ideas on how to prevent that, and how it is possible to return the plant's performance to its former glory.

If you work in an organization that has been very successful, and you don't think there is much room for improvement, reading these experiences and lessons learned will be a waste of your time. Just last week, I met the CEO of an extremely successful company. He told me that he really didn't feel there was much improvement needed because they were making record profits and producing better quality products than they had ever made in the history of their company. When I toured the plant, I saw a workforce that was totally unengaged. There was no shop floor discipline. Everyone I talked to complained about their working conditions and how "all this company cares about is profits". Their safety record was terrible, and the workforce/management relations were extremely adversarial. In my opinion, there is lots of room for improvement. However, they will never achieve it because the mission/vision/expectations of leadership has already been accomplished.

On the other hand, if your organization has some room to improve, or if you personally want to improve your management abilities, you might just get a few ideas from continuing on through the following pages.

"No one has more trouble than the person who claims to have no trouble"
-- **Taiichi Ohno**

Terry Offerle

02 May 2019

Lessons that need chapters:

- Simplicity is the key to efficient manufacturing operations
- We are in the people business
- We're not here to make friends – if you want a friend, get a dog
- The fundamentals of manufacturing
- How to and how not to treat people
- You have a jersey
- Don't crush creativity by telling everyone what to do step by step, but……
- Have and communicate a clear mission/direction that is not negotiable
- The Balanced Scorecard
- Failures are learning experiences that should be expected and celebrated
- What you do doesn't matter as much as how you do it.
- When you "get it", it's no longer what we do, it's who we are.
- Bobby Knight – "Your players will be satisfied with the level of performance you tolerate"
- Summary

1. Lesson learned – Simplicity is the key to efficient manufacturing operations

I was a witness to my company wasting millions of dollars on some of the world's most expensive computer systems that were going to solve all of our performance issues – multiple times!

I have worked with literally hundreds of manufacturing operations over my career from engine parts plants to pharmaceuticals manufacturers. I have not yet been able to understand why all of these companies have fallen for the pitch that they need to spend millions on these complicated scheduling systems to tell them what to make and when to make it. I truly believe that companies design these systems to be so difficult to understand that you need to hire them for support for the life of the system. And, after paying millions, they tell you if you ever want to get the upgrades to their systems, you cannot customize it at all. What???? Pay millions of dollars for a scheduling system that you can't modify to fit your business? Change my manufacturing processes so I can make your scheduling systems work??? Who is supporting who here???? And, if you buy all that, could I interest you in some oceanfront lots in Ohio?

The other fallacy that I have seen with these so called ERP systems is one of "common tools". This is the idea that we can justify the abhorrent costs of such systems because all of the company's plants will be on the same system and speak the same language. All plants will have the same reporting and doing things like forecasting, performance reporting, financial reports and month end close, would all be a breeze. Never seen it happen. If you have just a few plants in your company, you don't need such a monster. If you have a lot of diverse plants, because you can't do any customizations, it's useless. So, to avoid customization and to get meaningful information, plants devise other "mini-systems" to get the information they need to run the plant, and then pull information from the mini-system to feed the monster the generic diet it requires.

The other reality I have witnessed is that every time top management of the Company changes, so does the direction on which ERP system is the preferred one. So that lofty goal of having all operations and all locations on the same system never happens. In my experience, it takes the average manufacturing plant 8 to 12 months to completely implement a system. And, all plants have some "difficulty" during the initial launch of the new system. These difficulties range from a few bugs to work through to a total meltdown. So, you never want to launch too many operations at the same time. By the time you get a number of plants converted, management changes, and so does the ERP direction.

One of my favorite "new system launch issues" is inventory. I've seen it happen at three different plants. Just prior to the launch, companies will do a physical inventory so they know exactly how much raw, WIP, and finished goods they have. But after the launch, that inventory will either grow, or shrink, sometimes by hundreds of thousands of dollars! How can that be??? The only thing that changed was the system the information was loaded into. But yet it happens. I have seen substantial financial hits taken to "reconcile" the new system inventory.

I don't want to suggest there is not a business out there that requires a computer driven scheduling systems. That operation probably exists. I'm just saying that in the hundreds of manufacturing operations that I have been involved with over the past 43 years, I have not found one. I also don't want to come across as anti-computer. I am all for using computer systems to aid and support the manufacturing operations. I am not a fan when "the system" becomes what we do, and we start changing the way we manufacture to support "the system". I believe you should really spend some time thinking about why you can't just make what your customer wants, when they want it.

Another fact that I have found rather humorous as I go to different companies is that at the top of the organization, the executives and high level managers – especially the IT folks – actually think their ERP systems work. It's only when you work your way down to the shop floor level that you find the "mini system", the "manual systems", and the "workarounds" that have been created so they can actually run production efficiently.

Many of us managers grew up in an environment where some sort of MRP or ERP system was the norm, and we just accept the fact that "the system" tells us what we should make and when. For those of you in small companies, you may be saying – what is he talking about? We do just make what the customer wants, when he wants it. However, for those of you that grew up in large companies, you know exactly what I am saying, don't you? You just take it for granted that changing the way we schedule the plant is a decision well above my pay grade, and/or a sacred cow that I'm not allowed to even think about changing.

Again, really investigate why you can't make what the customer wants, when he wants it. My guess is you will find that the only thing standing in your path is your own inabilities. Some of those inabilities are perceived, and not real. You have been told for so long that "we can't do that", that you have come to believe it. Other inabilities are real, and in order to eliminate them, it will take real work that is sometimes very hard. One of the classics is set-up time. "I can't make what the customer wants when he wants it because I would have to make ten times as many set-ups as I do now".

Let me share a true story. We used to have minimum order quantities for all of our customers. Why? Because we couldn't make the set-ups that would be required if we let the customers buy the small quantities that they would like to buy, and still deliver on time. My boss came to me one day and said, "effective Monday, I am informing our Sales Department that our plant will no longer have minimum orders. I am doing this because I believe we will gain lots of new customers and eventually will increase our total demand." I told him to be prepared for past due orders and unhappy customers, because there is no way we can make that many set-ups. He told me that I needed to study up on S.M.E.D. and get busy reducing my set-up times. I told him that I had some training in S.M.E.D., and would do that, but why not give me some time to get better at set-ups before eliminating the minimums? He said, "Because that would take away your incentive to take set-up time reduction seriously".

The fact is, he was right. We had been "working on" S.M.E.D. for years and had shown only very slight improvements. We reported on that slight improvement each week, but there was no real pressure to do more, or go faster. When he removed the minimums, we had all the incentive (pressure) we needed. Our customers started to take advantage of the ability to order smaller quantities, and we got serious about set-up time reduction. We worked some long days, and missed a few on-time shipments, but we made more progress with set-up time reduction, in a shorter time frame, than I ever would have thought possible.

So, the lesson I learned: When the method of sequencing orders through the shop is a direct reflection of the customer demand, and the systems used are understandable, and make sense to the majority of the people on the shop floor, the need for ERP systems, a bunch of schedulers or expediters, hot lists, and IT personnel, are greatly reduced if not totally eliminated.

Every operation is different, and requires its own evaluation and investigation, and will require different actions to be taken. But the goal is the same: Make what the customer wants, when they want it.

2. We are in the people business

I started to learn this lesson a very long time ago, but I have to admit, it has only been in recent years that I fully appreciated how true and how important this lesson is.

I titled this chapter the way I did because a former boss of mine used to say it all the time. Many times, when issues would arise, Greg would say: "We may work in operations, but almost every time we face problems and issues we are reminded that we are in the people business". Truer words may never have been spoken.

If there is one statement I can make with certainty, it is that the success or failure you experience in a career in operations management is directly proportionate to the degree to which you understand human relationships. Your ability to work with people, and to allow them to bring out their best performance, whether they report to you or not, will determine the level of success you can attain in your career.

I will share several lessons learned by relating true stories about real people and situations that have taken place in my career. I won't use the people's names for obvious reasons, but I promise you each story is true and told as it happened.

First, let me give an opinion that will not be popular with some executive types. I do not believe that anyone in an operational management career should ever hold a position higher than "first line supervisor" unless they have first been a first line supervisor, for a minimum of two years. For me, it is just as important (in this line of work) as a formal education or any other work experience. You show me a first line supervisor with two or more years of experience, and I will show you someone that has learned to deal with all kinds of people and all kinds of situations. If that experience includes working shifts other that the day shift, double its value. No other experience or education will prepare you better for the situations you will face as a manager as you move up the chain of command. You will deal with people that are happy, mad, disgruntled, euphoric, cheaters, tattle tales, suck-ups, deviants, back stabbers, admirers, devil worshipers, born again believers, and practically anything else you can imagine. You will have to deal with the person that just lost a loved one. You will interact with someone that just won the lottery or some other fantastic situation. You will need to respond appropriately when someone is injured on the job, and you will respond when two of your employees get in a physical confrontation. And that's just in your first couple days!

Everyone doesn't want to be asked nicely. When I started my first week as a production supervisor, I was a little nervous. I was just 20 years old, and most of the people I was supervising were at least twice my age. There was this fork truck driver that was the grouchiest old fart I had ever met. He always had a scowl on his face, and rarely said anything, but when he did it was a grouchy or smart mouthed word or two. Someone had placed two containers of parts in a place where they didn't belong, and I knew that this fork truck driver (we'll call him Ron) was not going to move them to their proper location unless I told him to. Needless to say, I was a bit nervous about the prospect of telling Ron what to do. Now, in the way of background, I was taking classes at the local branch campus of Purdue University, and had taken several classes related to Supervision, Human Resource Management, and Organizational Behavior. So from a textbook perspective, I knew how I should approach him. Treat him as you would want to be treated, right? So, I walk up to Ron and I say: Ron, do you see those two bins over there? (He just looked at the bins and didn't answer) Would you please take them over to the plating machine and put them where they should be? Ron looked at me with that that usual scowl, looked at the two bins, and drove away without saying a word. About an hour passed, and I noticed the bins had not moved. I was a little perturbed at this point, but didn't want to have a confrontation, so I went to find Ron. When I found him, I again asked him, very politely, to take the bins to the plating machine. He again gave me the scowl, and drove away. Disappointed that I didn't get a response, I decided to give him a few minutes to see if he was going to move the bins. With every minute that went by, I became even angrier. After about 15 minutes, and the bins still sitting there, I was furious, and went to find Ron. When I found him, I lit into him with, "I want those bins taken to the plater, I want it done now, and I am not going to tell you again!" Ron broke into this big smile, and said, "That's more like it – now you sound like a real supervisor". Over time I learned that what Ron was doing was playing his little game that he played with all new supervisors to see how they would react to him. He knew I was nervous, and he saw his little game as a way to "break me in". He and I became good friends over time. He was a World War II veteran that had seen some very tough duty in the war. He was a very simple but very tough guy with a personality like no one I had met at that point in my life. He said I handled my first few days really well compared to some that were "afraid" of him. He said they didn't deserve to be supervisors if they wouldn't stand up to people like him.

I started at the plant as a press operator. I worked the day shift for several months, mainly for training, and then was transferred to the midnight shift. Like many others, I used to call anything other than first shift, the "off shifts". Many people still do, but when you work that shift, you don't see anything "off" about it, and you actually resent it when you are referred to as an "off shift employee". It's something I have been sensitive to ever since those days on third.

It was on third shift that I had the best supervisor ever and the worst supervisor ever. I learned a ton from both of them – what to do, and what not to do.

Rich was my first supervisor on third, and a guy that I have used, and still use today as the example of what a supervisor should be. He was the best. Of course like a lot of things, I appreciate the job he did more and more as the years went by, more than I did at the time.

Rich owned third shift. It was his. You were his. On the first day on third, he met with me and explained his expectations. If you had a question, or a problem, you went to Rich. Otherwise, you were expected to be at your machine and working. Breaks were 10 minutes – not 11. Lunch was 20 minutes – not 21. You were expected to be at your machine and working until 2 minutes before quitting time, and then you could wash up.

It was clear on third that these expectations of his were taken seriously. Not many people tested his expectations during my time there, but those that did, quickly and efficiently got a trip to the office and a reprimand on their permanent record. Rich would walk past my machine about 20 times each night, and every time he did, he noticed things. One time he came up and said, "Hey, there's some oil on the floor behind your press. You need to get that cleaned up". The next time it was, "your spacing between your parts is too wide and you're wasting coil – get that tightened up a little". It got to be a game. Every pass by was a chance for him to find something I could improve on. When he came by and didn't find anything, you just got this funny smile that said – I don't see anything this time – nice job, but I'll be back later.

If I could clone the supervisor that he was, I would buy a thousand of them. The guy was awesome. Why? He was firm, but fair. He was a trainer and coach that made you a better employee. He was nice, but always challenged you to be better. He took ownership and responsibility for his people and saw everything that happened on his shift as a reflection on him and his performance.

As often happens when someone does very well in a position, Rich was promoted to a first shift position, and I got a new boss – Willy. Willy was the polar opposite of Rich. He had been a supervisor for 30 years and if the truth be known, I think they put him on third with the hope he would retire. Well, he did, but he didn't leave the job. He was a 30 year supervisor with a bad attitude. He was pushed from one department and shift to another. His poor attitude rubbed off on those around him and he turned good workers into mediocre workers, and mediocre workers in poor employees. He had no idea and seemed not to care if his shift performed well or not. For the last several months that I worked under him, I was a "Leadperson", which is basically an hourly paid working foreman. He would be there at the shift startup, but within 10 minutes of the shift start, he would come to me and say, "Call me if anything happens that I need to know about". Then he would disappear for the rest of the shift. That was the norm. Very seldom did we see him at all during the shift. Employees did only as much work as they had to. Most employees left early and came back late for breaks and lunches. Some did very little work all night long. I learned that the few poor performers were quick to take advantage of the fact that there was no supervision and therefore no discipline. Then the average employees got the attitude that, why should I work if those guys aren't working. Even the good employees would underperform because they didn't want to take grief from the others. Third shift went from the best performers of all three shifts, to the worst by far. Willy knew this, and was actually hoping they would fire him so he could collect severance pay, which would be a sizable chunk after his 30 years.

There are actually multiple lessons learned in the above. One is the great example that Rich was as a supervisor. If you manage people, you could learn a lot from him. Be fair with your people but also be firm. Find a way, as he did, to enable and encourage people to do their best because THEY WANT TO, not because you will punish them if they don't. Most employees will respect a supervisor that challenges them to be a better performer, especially if they feel you acknowledge them for improving, and if he does it in a way that is not insulting or demeaning, and act more as a trainer and coach.

There are some obvious lessons learned from Willy as well. Just because you are good buddies with the people that work for you, that doesn't mean they will do good work for you. People usually tend to be satisfied with meeting your expectations. Rich's expectations were very high and most people tried very hard to meet them. Willy had very low expectations of his team, and they met them as well.

Probably the biggest lesson I learned from Willy was that we should never keep an employee that has lost their motivation and/or has a poor attitude about their job. It is poisonous and contagious. It spreads like wildfire, and destroys whatever gets in its path. An effort should have been made to correct Willy's performance, and if it didn't improve quickly and substantially, he should have been fired. I have seen this phenomenon before. For some reason a long time employee gets an attitude, and management feels they can't do anything about it. If you find yourself in this situation, don't assume the above is true. Make every attempt to turn around this negative attitude, and get them to an acceptable level of performance. If that isn't possible, talk to your HR professionals and determine if there is "cause" to terminate the employee's employment. If so, there may not be a legal requirement to pay any, or at least full severance. Even if severance is required, the costs of keeping the manager with a poor attitude and poor performance also need to be considered as part of the decision.

Hopefully, there are not too many people like Willy that are reading this book. My hope is that most of you are reading this with the idea that you may read a nugget or two that will help you be just a little bit better manager. But, if you identify with Willy at all, please do yourself and your employer a huge favor....

Stop it. If you are that unhappy with your job, if you dislike the company that you work for that much, if going to work makes you that miserable, if you can no longer feel good about positive improvements and accomplishments in your work, then leave – find another job. Staying in that type of a situation helps no one. It is bad for your health and wellbeing, and it is insuring a poor work record which you may need someday. Just get out of that situation, and find a job where you can contribute to a company and reach your personal and professional objectives.

3. We're not here to make friends...... If you want a friend, get a dog

I was not present when it took place, so I am unable to confirm it as fact. However, the very popular rumor in our company is that when one senior manager said something about being friends with a co-worker, the non-executive Chairman of the company responded with the title of this chapter.

While I certainly don't want to come across as being quite that harsh, there is a nugget of importance there that should be mined.

My first job as a supervisor came after being an hourly paid, rank and file machine operator in the same department. So, many of my coworkers became my direct reports. For a period of several months, this felt very awkward. However, over time I found that some of my, so called, friends would try to take advantage of the relationship, thinking that I would not hold them accountable to the "rules". This was not a big issue because as an hourly employee, they knew me as someone that obeyed the rules and always did his best to perform acceptably.

I can't really recall at what point in my career this changed, but over time, I realized there was a clear line that needs to be drawn between personal relationships and business relationships. That is NOT to say that you can't be friends with people that, directly or indirectly, work for you. It does however mean that BOTH PARTIES need to understand that the personal relationships must not impinge on the professional relationship and vice versa. As mentioned above, the employee may abuse the relationship by expecting his/her personal friend to allow them a little more freedom to stretch the rules, or "turn their head" to small violations. But I have also seen abuse in the other direction. The supervisor/manager may feel more comfortable throwing those undesirable tasks and crappy assignments to his/her "friend" who may be more likely to do it without complaining or arguing with their pal.

When I was a new employee, as I suspect most new employees do, I watched my co-workers to see what they did. When you're the "new guy", you want to fit in. You don't want to be seen by management as someone that "stands out", at least not at first. You want management to believe that they made a good choice when they hired you, and you want to be seen as a "good worker". On the other hand, you didn't want your peers to think you were trying to "suck up" by going too far above and beyond the call of duty. By the end of my first week, I was doing pretty well at the few tasks that I had been trained on. I was working hard at getting better, and didn't realize that my output was beginning to be well above average. At that point, I didn't even know what average was. One of the "old timers" in the department that had been one of my trainers earlier in the week came over and gave me some advice. He said, "What are you trying to do, make the rest of us look bad?" At first, I honestly didn't have a clue about what he was talking about. He then pointed to the parts counter on the machine, pointed to his watch, gave me a look that ran a chill down my back, and walked away. I got it. I learned that if you want to fit into the culture, there is a balance that most employees fall into. You perform just well enough to keep your supervisor happy, but not so well that you draw the ire of your co-workers. It's an interesting concept that is really just part of normal human behavior. Later, when I started taking some college courses in Organizational Behavior and Psychology, I was surprised to learn that most of my instructors had only a superficial and very academic understanding of how prevalent and important it is for a future manager to understand these interpersonal relationships and the psychology behind them.

I also observed another interesting trap that far too many supervisors and managers fall into. One of my co-workers – Kenny - was a great guy and a great worker. He always had a smile on his face, and seemed to be thrilled to have a job, no matter what the job was. If there was a crappy job to be done, when you were chosen to do it, you, like most, would bitch, moan, and complain, and try to come up with some lame excuse why you shouldn't have to do it and someone else should. Not Kenny. No matter how rotten the task, Kenny would respond with a smile and get busy. Because of Kenny's great attitude and demeanor, he was repeatedly abused by multiple supervisors. It was way easier to ask Kenny to do it, than to argue with some grouch, or worse, one of your "friends". Of course, it was outrageously unfair and abusive for Kenny to make him work harder, longer, and under worse working conditions than the other employees, but it made the life of the supervisor much easier.

Don't think for a second that this only happens at the machine operator level of a company. I have seen the exact same phenomenon in high level managers who find it so much easier to throw more and more work onto the subordinate that will just work harder and longer to get it done, than to others that will complain and expect a raise and/or promotion in return for the slightest of extra effort.

Don't be that manager. Spread the undesirable tasks around. Be an equal opportunity delegator when it comes to balancing the workload. Expect a high level of performance from all of your direct reports, not just the ones that will do their best without hesitation. And even more importantly, reward that exceptional performance when you have the opportunity.

I have worked with very few managers that were capable of completely separating the personal from the business relationships. Most of us think we can do it, but we are really not that good at it. It is human nature to treat your friends with more tolerance than the average employee with whom you don't have a personal relationship. So, the moral of the story..... Don't get too close personally with those you supervise directly, or indirectly.

I once had a supervisor James, who really struggled with this idea of personal/professional separation. Among his direct reports was: Chuck, whom he despised. Chuck was that contrary person who wanted to argue with everything. He was not a good worker, and spent most of his time causing trouble by playing games with people's minds. Also reporting to James was Rick. Rick was a close friend to James, and they spent a lot of their time together outside of work. They were hunting and fishing partners, and the friendship went back years.

One day, James caught Chuck reading a "Hot Rod" magazine when he should have been working. He immediately brought him to the office and proceeded to formally reprimand him. Within minutes of getting his reprimand, we received a grievance from the union charging the supervisor with harassment and favoritism. The grievance specifically named Rick and someone that routinely reads magazines while he is supposed to be working, but "that's OK with James because Rick is his buddy". When the HR Manager showed the grievance to me, we decided to take a walk out to James's department. When we walked up to the area where Rick normally works, he was there, not working, and reading an issue of Field and Stream Magazine. What was even more disturbing was James was standing less than twenty feet away from him, but didn't even notice that he was reading the magazine. Needless to say, we conceded the grievance, and Chuck's reprimand was rescinded from his record. James also received some one on one "training" on being a professional manager and how all rules apply to all employees, not just the ones that you want to apply them to.

Even if you are really good at separating the two relationships, the perception of others in the organization will most likely not agree that you treat everyone the same. In these cases, perception is no different than reality. If you and Joe both report to me, but you know that at least once per week, I have lunch with Joe, and I have never invited you to go to lunch…….

My perception is that, when we are "on the job", I treat both of you the same. Is that your perception?

Just a side note regarding James... In a later chapter, I will talk about the right and the wrong way to hire people. Nothing against James personally, but he was a good example of hiring someone for all of the wrong reasons. Back "in the day", it was very popular to promote your best set-up person to be the supervisor. The reasoning being that they knew the machines, parts, and processes best, and could get the most efficiency from the process. They knew how to "get a lot of parts made". While that was true, what was not recognized at the time was that the key to long term success and profitability was much more complicated than just making a lot of parts. By the time we realized that what we needed in a supervisor was not just the ability to make the machines go fast, but also a manager , trainer, coach, developer, teacher, of people and processes, we had many people in the job that were not capable. James was one of these. If the machine malfunctioned, James could fix it. But he had very little skill in quality management, scheduling, finance and almost no skill at all when it came to the interaction or communication, let alone management, of people. Almost every time he had to interact with people, which by the way was the biggest part of his job, it ended with less than desirable and sometimes disastrous results. James was not an isolated case. I met and worked with many managers that got into their positions because they were the best "set-up person". This is still an ongoing problem today. As a matter of fact, I believe it is making a comeback. In this age of struggling to find good qualified candidates, companies are compromising their standards and again hiring people that clearly do not meet the qualifications for the position in an effort to get the position filled quickly. The best set-up person, someone that is perceived as being "a good worker", or a friend or relative that someone thinks "can do the job", is being placed in jobs that they do not have the skills, abilities, aptitude, experience, or education for.

Don't for a minute think that this only happens in the production supervisor area. As a matter of fact I think it is actually a major problem with compensation systems and policies in many companies today.

Here's an example:

I used to work with a brilliant engineer. He graduated at the top of his engineering school and went on to do great things in his field by designing machines and tools, solving complex quality problems, and developing new products. But because he had been promoted to the highest pay grade we had for engineering positions, the only way for him to be promoted again was to make him a manager. So he was promoted to Engineering Manager. In less than one year after his promotion, he was fired for poor performance. Why? Because we took him away from everything he was good at, and gave him a position where his primary job was to manage people – an area where he had zero education, zero experience, zero aptitude, and zero chance of being successful.

After being terminated at our company, he went to work as an engineer at another company and enjoyed a long and successful career at what he was good at.

Another "relationship" disaster is relatives supervising relatives. It NEVER works. Under no circumstances should you allow a manager to supervise one of their relatives – directly or indirectly. Just as the above example, even if they can separate the personal from the professional, the perception issues that it creates are not worth the risks. Even in the best situations, it creates hard feelings among the other non-related workers, within the family, or both.

Again, I have seen example after example of issues that took up manager's time and made us less efficient because of family conflicts. There was the supervisor that didn't take the disciplinary action he should have because the employee was the son of another supervisor in a different department, and he didn't want him to hold it against him. There was the accounting clerk that was disrespectful to some of the engineers because she knew they received better raises than her husband who was also an engineer. There was the inspector that got very angry every time she saw her supervisor husband communicate with other female workers in his area of responsibility, especially the good looking ones. There was the constant friction of the purchasing manager that used to be the sister-in-law to the quality manager before he cheated on her sister. I could go on and on with this list. Again, if you can possibly avoid it, avoid it.

In smaller, family owned businesses, having a no-relation policy may not be practical. However, every effort should be made to hire the best candidate available whenever there is an opening. If the best available candidate just happens to be a relative and it is not feasible to arrange it so they report to someone else, be very conscious of the potential problems your decision will bring, and be prepared to deal with them.

So, what is the lesson learned here? I have heard it said many, many times during the course of my career that "every manager has or will develop their own style". My feeling is that if you truly have just one "style of management" you will never be completely successful as a manager. The reason I feel this way is because the operations manager needs to be able to deal effectively with all types of situations, and all types and personalities of people. In school they referred to it as being the "situational manager". It is my experience that the most successful managers are those that can very quickly and accurately assess the situation and people they are dealing with, and then choose the appropriate "style of management" to arrive at the optimal result.

If you have been asked to implement a new quality policy in your operation, the best result may be to first meet with the quality manager. You would want him to be the champion of this implementation, so a good first step would be to meet and review the new policy to make sure you both understand it the same way, and are on the same page regarding the need for the new policy. Then you would want to discuss how we proceed with the implementation, and probably suggest that the management team will need to be consulted, and they too must be on board with the need for, and process of the implementation. Your role in this process would be to support the quality manager's efforts, and to encourage the involvement of as many people as possible in the implementation, as well as regular follow-up with the quality manager for progress status.

On the other hand, if there is a fire reported in a section of the plant, you are not going to schedule a meeting, or form a committee to discuss what steps should be taken next.

In the case of the new quality policy, you might say the best "management style" would be participative, and serve as more of a facilitator and coach. However, when there's an emergency that needs to be dealt with immediately and decisively, you must quickly switch to an authoritarian style of leadership, and make some things happen now, without much discussion or debate.

Those of you that are experienced operations managers know that these are two very extreme examples, and the "style" of leadership for these examples is pretty obvious. However, you also know that there are hundreds of situations that happen every day where you have to make a call about how you will react and what management style you will use, and always choosing the right approach is very much easier to talk about than it is to do. If you stay in the "authoritarian" mode too often, eventually you will fail as a manager. But calling meetings and forming teams is certainly not always the best approach either. Sometimes you must take a hard line approach. Sometimes you need to walk away and let the issue be dealt with by someone at a lower level in the organization. There are hundreds of options that fall somewhere between these two extremes, and they are not always obvious.

Don't be discouraged when you take the wrong approach, because you will. I and every good manager I have ever known have made many bad calls in this area. When you realize that you should have taken a different tact, chalk it up to experience, and try to learn from your mistake moving forward. You will get better at it with experience. Remember, everyone is different, and may react differently to different styles of management. So, even the exact same situation may call for a different management style, depending on the individuals involved.

The management of people is not an exact objective science. It is full of variables that are constantly changing, and to be an effective leader, the operations manager must be knowledgeable and quick to recognize those changes, but also nimble, with the ability change and adapt to those changes in a way that produces the best possible outcomes.

4. The Fundamentals of Manufacturing

Have you ever heard a coach tell his players to go out there and play your best, but keep one eye on the scoreboard at all times? I doubt it. What you probably have heard coaches say is that we need to master the fundamentals of the game. In football, the fundamentals are blocking, tackling, passing, kicking, and running. There are many variations and techniques of these fundamentals that the coaches will drill and drill during practice after practice. When game day comes, the coach will tell his player that they need to go out on the field, on every play, and concentrate on perfect execution of the fundamentals on every down. And, if they do that, the scoreboard will take care of itself.

So what are the fundamentals? You have to define them. It is my opinion that most of them are the same, regardless of the business you're in. However, there is room for some discretion depending on the type of business you're in, and what the objectives of the business are. For example, the fundamentals for a not for profit business could be different than that of a highly competitive business that has to improve profits to survive.

The fundamentals are not a ten page listing of everything that you would like to see the business accomplish. It is a one page listing of bullet points – somewhere between five and twenty. It is the essentials of how the business will be run. It is the firm and non-negotiable rules that we can go to for the bottom line answer when there is a question. It is not only what we do, it is who we are. It MUST be simply stated, easy for all to understand, and leaves no room for interpretation.

While we like initiative, creativity, new ideas, and innovation in all other aspects our business, the fundamentals are NOT NEGOTIABLE.

I have worked with many companies, including my own, whose manufacturing fundamentals were changed like a pair of dirty socks. Every time there was a significant change in leadership, there was a change in how the business was run. I'm sure you have heard of the "program of the month" that was going to be the answer to all of our issues. You get a new CEO and he is a fan of Six Sigma. So that's the route you take for a while. You spend a fortune and invest millions to send people to training and get certifications. Then along comes a new operations manager that believes an investment in a new ERP computer system that ties together a shop floor control system, a quality system, an HR system, and a finance system will bring us to the pinnacle of state of the art technology. So we start training and implementation, but after two plants, realize that it is costing 5 times what it was supposed to and taking 3 times longer to implement, so we scrap the idea due to lack of funding. Then upper management decides that we need some outside help so they hire a large management consulting firm that promises to deliver tens of millions in savings. They send in scores of consulting associates that have never held a real manufacturing position and been held accountable to a P&L for more than a year or two at best. They have however spent decades in colleges and universities either as a professional student, or as a professor. And, chances are, they have written at least two books! But after 18 months or so, you realize that you have paid out over a million dollars for their help, and you have seen little if any performance improvement. Of course the reason you haven't seen the improvement is because YOUR PEOPLE have failed to implement the techniques and processes that they brought them. Your analysis of the resultant savings is drastically different than their calculations, so there is a huge disagreement as to what is owed them. After they threaten a law suit, you end up deciding to agree on a settlement somewhere in the middle, and terminate their services immediately.

I know that some of you are laughing as you read this because you think I just described your company. All of the above actually happened in a company that I worked for – multiple times! – And I know other companies that did the same.

I believe that it really does not matter what your fundamental system of manufacturing – the way you chose to run your operation – is. I believe that any manufacturing system will be a resounding success if:

1. You clearly define the manufacturing fundamentals
2. You do not compromise the fundamentals – not negotiable
3. You stick to it – make it who you are not what you do and don't change every time the wind blows from a different direction
4. You insure every employee is on board with the fundamentals or leaves the organization
5. You hire the right people for the right positions, and retain them (that's another whole chapter)
6. Management is passionate about where they are taking the organization from the top down through all levels

Let's talk about the management team at the plant level. By management team, I am referring to the Plant Manager and his direct reports. The dynamics of the relationships among this group are both complex and interesting, and can determine the plant's success or failure. I could write another entire chapter on this group, but for the purposes of this chapter, I'll be brief.

First and foremost, the plant manager has two critical responsibilities as it relates to the fundamentals:

1. Establish the fundamentals for your plant, communicate them in a way that no employee at any level can say they weren't aware, or didn't understand them, and continually reinforce them.
2. Strictly enforce adherence to the fundamentals, without exception, and take swift and substantial appropriate action with anyone that violates them.

All other members of the management team also have two critical responsibilities:

1. Strictly adhere and support the fundamentals, and educate the workforce on the need and reasons why the fundamentals are important and cannot be compromised.
2. If for any reason you can't support, or feel a modification is necessary to the fundamentals, immediately discuss the situation with the Plant Manager, and no one else.

The management team MUST be of one voice when it comes to how the plant will be managed. In management team meetings, behind closed doors, all opinions and ideas can and should be openly discussed. However, at the end of the meeting, before leaving the room, the management team must all be in the same boat, and rowing in the same direction.

When that new plant manager came to our struggling plant and made substantial and immediate improvement, it was not the lean techniques and knowledge of how to implement that made him successful, even though that is exactly what we believed at the time. The key to that success was that he brought something far more important. He brought, and communicated, where we were going to take the plant, and exactly how we were going to get there, in a way that everyone could understand.

Read on……

5. How To and How Not To Treat People

So everyone thinks they know how to and how not to treat people, right? That may be true when talking about the relationship between just two individuals – you and one other. However, when you are a manager of people, it's never just two people in the equation. And let's also face reality – and that is there is no objective measure for how you treat people – it is all a perception. How you perceive you are treating someone may be quite different from how they perceive they are being treated. That perception is derived from a very complex set of variable inputs. To illustrate just a few, consider the following:

Supervisor: Woke up in his beautiful home, next to his beautiful wife, showered in his new personal spa, climbed in his new SUV, stopped at Starbucks for a caramel latte and a Wall Street Journal, cruised into the office, checked the headlines and a couple emails, then headed out to the shop floor.

Subordinate: Forgot to set the alarm and overslept, quickly throws on yesterday's clothes and splashes some water on his face, remembers that his recent divorce has left him with a car that only starts when it wants to and realizes there is no way to get to work on time, but tries anyway, only to get stopped for speeding on the way to work, where his pay will be docked for the 15 minutes that he is late.

I will let your imagination fill in the potential outcomes of any interactions these two people will have this morning. They have many varied inputs into their current state, and are at opposite ends of the emotional spectrum. No matter what happens next, and no matter what someone says, there will be two very different perceptions of reality. But this is normal. This is real. And, you can multiply this times the number of people working in the area.

So when the manager makes a decision, and gives guidance and direction to the employee, there can easily be at least two completely different opinions of how that person was treated. But it's not just them. Everyone around them that realizes the two have had an interaction also has a perception of how each of them was treated, as does the supervisor's boss. And, many more people will also form a perception of how they were treated as the two of them tell others throughout the day how they were treated by the other.

The lesson here is that managers need to be professionals. They need to conduct themselves at all times in a professional manner. It is very easy for a manager to stray off the professional path, and everyone does it from time to time, but be careful. Recognize when it happens, and get back on track quickly.

Remember the third shift supervisor that wanted to be everyone's buddy? He would joke around with the guys. He would hang out with them at the bar after work. He was just "one of the guys". By the time he realizes that his subordinates have absolutely no respect for his position as a supervisor, he is totally ineffective as a leader. How do you think he is perceived by the workers? By his peers? By his boss? I'm sure there is almost no one that feels that he treats people in a professional manner.

I have had supervisors tell me that they don't feel comfortable being too strict about enforcing the rules. They are concerned that "they have to work with these people every day". In my opinion, that comment is a supervisor that doesn't want to do the job he is being paid to do, and he needs to find a new line of work. Enforcing the rules doesn't mean you are mistreating anyone. Enforcing rules is not personal or emotional. You don't need to be disrespectful to enforce rules and policies. As a matter of fact, if you do your job professionally, you will take the responsibility for making sure your employees understand not only what the rules are, but why they are important. Make your expectations crystal clear to everyone, and let them know that you are charged with the responsibility to insure rules and policies are adhered to. Let them know that you are available to discuss any questions or concerns regarding the rules and policies. And, make sure they understand that a big part of your job is to provide all the tools and assistance possible to insure THEY can be successful. After that, if they choose to abuse them, you should not have reason to feel bad about taking the necessary action with them.

The key here is that no matter what the employee has done, or how they choose to conduct themselves, the manager must treat the employee in a professional way, with respect and dignity. Remember, your objective is to provide the opportunity for the employee to improve their performance and make him/her a better employee. That is why there are typically progressive steps in the disciplinary process – to give the employee every opportunity to improve.

I have said many times, and I still firmly believe that no one should ever be surprised when they lose their job. If it is a job elimination situation, those don't happen overnight. They take time to plan and organize. There is no good reason not to give the displaced employee plenty of notice and an opportunity to look for a new position. If it is for performance reasons, there should have been multiple performance reviews with clearly spelled out objectives, to give the employee time to turn their performance around. They should also have been told what would happen if the performance did not improve. And finally, if an employee commits an act that results in immediate termination, they should have been informed of the penalty for such acts, and therefore shouldn't be surprised at the result.

People can be taught some of the specific things that make a good manager and leader, but I truly believe that to be a good manager and leader, you have to have a passion for people. You have to want to see others succeed. When I think about the people in my career that I believe to be great managers, they all had a true desire to help me, and others, be successful. If the only person that you have a burning desire to see succeed is yourself, you may want to consider another line of work.

I would now like to introduce all of you that are currently in positions responsible for hiring people, to your biggest obstacle to getting the right people hired. Stand up. Go find a mirror, and take a good long gander into it. Right now, all of the HR Managers are saying, yep, he's right. Those operations managers make terrible hiring decisions. And, the operations managers are saying the same thing about the HR Managers. I'm convinced that is the reason some companies involve so many people in the hiring process. So, months from now, when it's clear we made a mistake, everyone has someone else to blame!!!

I'm sure there are some companies out there that do it right and rarely make a bad choice. But they must be the same companies that really need a huge complicated ERP system, because I haven't found them either. I'm partially joking, but not completely. Way too often, we hire people for positions for all of the wrong reasons. For example: Has anyone seen a hire because…….

- We needed someone quickly and he was available and could start right away and already knows the people and the department
- He's a close friend of the boss, and has his full support for the position
- He's young and eager, and we need some new blood in the organization
- She's never going to leave here, so we can get her for less money, and won't have to worry about replacing her in a couple years
- Her dad works here and he has been an excellent worker for the past 40 years, so she comes from a good family and has a good work ethic
- I think the rest of the team would really like working with her
- His background, education, and experience are just like mine…..
- He is really tight with the head of our division, so he will be able to get some influence on decisions in our favor

Believe it or not, I have actually seen people hired with all of the above being the statement that resolved which of the candidates would be chosen for the position. I could also share twice that many examples where people were NOT considered for positions, and eliminated from the candidates list, for even dumber reasons (wearing clothes to the interview that were out of style, physical appearance, the college they attended didn't measure up, arrived at the interview five minutes late, didn't bring paper and pen to take notes). There is a better way, but it will only work if everyone involved in the process agrees to take a disciplined approach.

First, when you believe you have an opening to fill, select the three best and most qualified people to be the hiring team. One of them must be a representative from HR, and one must be the manager that the new person will report to. The third can be chosen by the other two, but should be someone that is most knowledgeable about the requirements and challenges of the open position.

The hiring team's first challenge is to determine if the position can be eliminated and not filled at all. If it is determined that it must be filled, they should determine "when". Is it urgent, or is there plenty of time? The process is the same regardless, but this step will give the team some guidance regarding the priority and sense of urgency that will need to be undertaken.

The next step is for the team to review the job description for the open position, if there is one, and if not, they must write a new one. This is the most critical step in the hiring process. If there is an existing job description, it probably needs to be re-written. The job description should be a detailed document that explains exactly what the PERFECT candidate would look like. It MUST include:

- Specific experience – not general experience – that the candidate should have and to what degree – what positions he would have held and for how many years.

- Degrees, milestones, awards, or certifications the perfect candidate would have achieved.
- The level of interpersonal skill that is required for the position.
- Your expectations for written and oral communication skills.
- Management style/personality traits that would be best for the position.
- Tendency towards conformance to norms, or an out of the box thinker.
- Change agent or supporter of current methods.
- Energy level and sense of urgency when needed.
- Self-motivation and ability to work independently with little to no supervision.
- Ability to be an effective team member that works well with others vs. the need to lead the team, and flexibility to do either as needed.
- Requirements for relocation and or travel
- Future promotion potential or someone that will be satisfied in the position long term
- Any other skills, traits, or expectations that you feel are important to the position.

At this point you have a document that describes your perfect candidate, and you can now start the search for that person. Understand that you will likely not find the "perfect candidate" that matches up exactly with the job description. However, using this description as a guide, you can objectively rate each candidate on what you have determined is most important in a candidate. The idea is that you will hire the person that comes closest to matching up with the description, instead of the wrong reasons listed above.

Develop a scorecard that lists the most important aspects of the job description. After each interview, rate the candidate on a 0 to 5 scale in each aspect. After all candidates are interviewed, this scorecard will be used to narrow the list, or possibly even select the right candidate.

In addition to taking some of the emotion out of the process, and making it more objective, following this process also provides another big advantage. It makes the process much more efficient. I have seen several companies lose some very talented candidates because they simply draw out the process for too long. They don't know exactly what they are looking for, they are not sure who needs to be involved, they haven't determined who will interview the candidates, and when they do, that person isn't available. After the interviews, they all have differing opinions about the candidates because there was no agreement on what they were looking for from the start. If it takes longer than three weeks from initial contact with a candidate to making an offer, odds increase significantly that another company will get an offer in their hands before you do.

Let me share a perfect example of what I'm talking about…..

A former mentee of mine recently contacted me about a position that he heard was opening up in a company where both of us used to work. He knows that I frequently do recruiting for this company, and wanted my help in being considered for the position. This guy is a top notch performer, and would be a huge asset to this company if they could land him, so I'm thinking this is going to be a breeze, a slam dunk that won't take any time to at all. Boy was I mistaken. I started with the Company's HR Director. We had a great conversation. He remembered the candidate from several years back, and told me that he was excited to have an opportunity to consider him for the position. He asked me to submit his resume, and said he would get with the Operations Director, and get the ball rolling. I reminded him that the candidate had been with his current employer for three years, and they had discussed his next career moves, but the right position just hadn't opened up for him. I made sure he knew that it could be much harder to get him if we waited until he was offered a nice promotion to stay with his current company. He agreed and again asked me to submit the resume, which I did the next day.

One week later, I had heard nothing. I again called the HR Director. He said that the Ops Director had taken a vacation, and it would be another week before they could talk. Trying not to sound too pushy, I again reminded him of the sense of urgency I felt we needed, and asked if he could do a phone interview with the candidate. He agreed, and said he would ask his secretary to check his calendar and set something up. Three days later, having heard nothing, I called his secretary. She told me that she didn't know there was any rush, and had scheduled the call for the following week. Fine, at least it was scheduled. That call happened went fine, and the next step would be a call with the Ops Director. The HR Manager had promised me that he would arrange it, but I decided to call the Ops Director anyway. He was surprised, because he didn't know we were considering a new candidate for the position, and said he would need to talk to the HR Director before he could agree to talk to the candidate. No, I'm not exaggerating! It took another week before we managed to get the candidate on a call with the Ops Director, but we finally did, and it went very well as we knew it would. The HR Director then informed me that we would now need to schedule a visit to the corporate headquarters so that both he and the VP of Operations could have a face to face meeting with the candidate. The problem, he explained, was going to be that next week is a Global Leadership Conference in Europe, and they both would be unavailable. And, the week after that, the VP of Operations would be in China for a week and a half, so we needed to look at dates THREE WEEKS OUT!!!! I told him that we needed to find an alternative plan or we would lose this candidate. All through this process I had been talking to the candidate, reassuring him that they really were interested in him. That everyone was just incredibly busy right now, and they were doing their best to make this happen. Each time I spoke with him, he seemed just a little less excited about the opportunity. He never said it, but I know he had to feel that they really didn't care about him. They certainly had no regard for his time, only for theirs. Two weeks later, while the VP was still in China, the candidate's current employer offered him a nice promotion that included some nice perks, a bigger salary and annual bonus, and a nice plush new office. During that same time, we did manage to get a phone call set up between the candidate and the VP of Operations, and as expected, that went very well, and suggested we go to the next step. Immediately after that call, I called the HR Director and left a message. I also sent an email saying that we needed to get an offer in the candidate's hands ASAP. Again, no call back or response to the email for another three days. He finally sent an email saying that he was on his way to South America, and would call me to discuss an offer as soon as he could. Unbelievable!

A few days later, the candidate informed me of the offer he had received. It was a similar position as we had talked to him about, and the compensation was much better than what we had discussed. He informed me that he was going to withdraw his candidacy for the new position, accept the offer, and stay with his current employer.

When I informed the VP of HR, he acted surprised and disappointed. He wanted to know if he would reconsider if they matched his new compensation package. I already knew the answer. It had nothing to do with compensation. He had formed an opinion of the culture of the company, and how employees are treated by the way he was treated as a candidate.

The sad part of this story is that it is NOT an isolated incident. Making candidates feel like inferior pests that are messing up their schedules by interrupting their routines with these stupid interviews, is really not all that unusual!!!!!

In the above case, it was two months from the time I initially submitted this candidate for consideration until his withdrawal. That is entirely too long to expect a candidate to wait that is truly ready for a career change. Companies need to develop a process for the recruiting, screening, selection, and hiring of new employees. I have described one such process above. Use that one or develop your own, but streamline your process, make it efficient, and put some discipline into it.

One of the most important jobs you have as a manager is to hire, develop, and retain outstanding human talent for your organization. That is a contribution you can make that will pay dividends back to the company for years to come. And, it can hurt your company for years to come if you do a poor job at it!

In the early days of my career, it was very difficult to find a good job. There was tremendous competition between candidates for the open position. If you advertised an opening for a manager position, you would expect to see 20 or 30 high quality applications within the week. Today's marketplace is the polar opposite. There are many more open positions out there than high quality candidates. Many of the people you are trying to attract are working for companies that recognize their value, and are taking steps – both traditional and non-traditional – to retain them. When those companies need to hire from outside, it is much easier because their current employees help to sell prospective employees on the company. You have to be the company that actively works at impressing the candidate. Make them feel that they are respected while going through the hiring process. Don't make them wait in the lobby for 15 minutes past the time you asked them to be there. It sends a message. Offer them a water or a coffee while you're talking with them. Never make them wait to see the next person who will talk to them. Personally introduce them to their next contact, and leave your number so they can call you with questions later. Offer to pay any expenses that were incurred as a result of the interview. Don't make them ask if they can be reimbursed and how to do it. Provide them with written information about the company, the benefits programs, and rules and policies rather than expecting them to remember everything they have heard during the course of the interviewing process. Show them that you are a company and a group of people that they would enjoy working with. How they are treated during the visit, and how comfortable they are with it, to many candidates is just as important, if not more so, than the compensation package.

I could write many more pages on recruiting and retention, and the good and bad examples that I have seen. But, I will sum it up by saying this...... Work every day at making your company a great place to work. All companies say that "people are our most important asset". In the companies that really believe it, they don't have to say it. Their employees already know it, and their policies, practices, and procedures reflect it.

6. You Have A Jersey

Have you ever tried out for a team sport? During "try-outs", no one gets a team uniform. In a best case, they may have some different colored shirts or vests so they can tell offense from defense. Only when you have proven yourself worthy – only when you have demonstrated that you are capable of playing at a level that will advance the team's performance – only when you have "made the team" do you get a jersey.

Typically, after try-outs are over, and the team has been formed, and the jerseys have been assigned, unless you do something really stupid, you no longer have to be worried about getting cut from the team. Once we are a team, we do what it takes to help and support each other in an effort to make sure the team is successful. We all have strengths and weaknesses, and we take advantage of that as a team. By being a part of the team, we are committing to each other that our overall success is more important than our individual achievements.

And so it must be in operational organizations.

I once had a boss whose motivational strategy was to give his direct reports impossible tasks and objectives. The idea being that even though he knew we could never achieve them, if we made it just half way to the objective, the result would be huge improvement from where we started and his superiors would see him as doing a great job. So every week, every month, and every quarter we were chastised, told we were performing poorly, threatened with poor performance evaluations, and verbally abused because we were behind the objectives. Then at the end of the year, we were told we did a good job for the year, and were recognized for the year over year improvement. But during the year, I certainly didn't feel as though I was part of a team. Each year, at least one of the other managers would leave the company. I felt zero loyalty to the organization because I felt zero loyalty from them. I wondered many times if they would make good on some of the threats, and replace me with someone that they felt could do a better job. Many times, I felt that I should quit too, but I guess the right opportunity didn't come along at the right time.

I can honestly tell you now that that those were the worst years of my career. Not only for me personally, but my personal performance suffered too. I was not motivated to do my best. Subconsciously, I knew that my performing better would just make my boss look better, and I really didn't want that. It was like telling an Olympic high jumper he has to jump 10 feet or he is worthless, when he knows the world record is 8 feet. What's the point in trying?

I read somewhere once that the single biggest reason that good people leave their jobs to seek other employment is not money, status, location, or title.... It is to get away from what they perceive to be a bad boss situation or simply a situation where they perceive they are not being treated well. While I believe that to be very true generally, there is an exception that is worth mentioning.

In the course of my career I once encountered a boss – my boss – that in my opinion was the worst excuse for a manager of people I had ever come across. I know of three individuals that left the company, only because of this manager. He had zero interpersonal skills, and treated his direct reports like they were put on this earth to carry out his wants and desires. However, the unfortunate reality was that he and the CEO of the company had a personal relationship that went back years. Because of this, his boss, his boss's boss, and the entire Human Resource Department was afraid to expose him for the total ass that he was. Many employees went to his boss and to the HR Department to complain about him. But nothing was done about the situation, and several more people left the company, took positions in other departments or divisions, or retired early just to get away from him. I am certain that if the CEO had known how terrible a manager he was, he would have removed him. But, the perception that he was "the boss's friend", made several in the organization afraid to do their jobs for fear of "getting on the wrong side of the boss". So, when people say that people don't leave companies, they leave bad bosses…….. If the company is aware of the bad boss, and multiple levels of managers choose not to deal with the situation, then it is not just the boss, it's a systemic problem in the company.

You get a jersey when you are on the same path. When your actions are always in the best interest of the team. When you understand your role, and you contribute your best every day to accomplishing the objectives of the team.

To be clear, this does NOT mean that once you have a jersey, you will always have the jersey. Just like in all high performance teams, you have to continue to perform at a high level as a team, and as an individual contributing to the team, to stay on the team. You must continually be looking for ways to improve the success of the team. When a teammate stumbles, you need to be there to prop him up. When you struggle, you need to ask your teammates for help.

Ever have a situation where there is a poor performer on your team and everyone knows it? Even after the best efforts of the manager and coworkers to help the person get better, they still performed poorly? Maybe it had gone on for so long that the employee was conditioned to believe there are no negative consequences to poor performance so why work hard and try? Were there statements made and positions taken to rationalize the decision to avoid dealing with the problem? "He has been here a long time, and he'll retire soon, so we'll get by". "His last three managers didn't deal with him, I can't start now"! "I think if I just stay after him about not performing well, he will eventually quit, and I won't have to deal with it." What if it were a professional championship team in the NFL? Do you think those players can get away with poor performance? Do you think it matters that they have been there a long time? Do you think the coaches will rationalize poor performance, and make excuses for the player that's not executing the fundamentals of the game the way he knows he should? I don't think so. What is the difference in this example and an employee or manager in a professional world class manufacturing operation? Is being successful on the football field more important than being successful in the manufacturing business? Just some food for thought.

I know that sports analogies can get tiring, but sometimes they are a great way to get people to easily understand a complex interpersonal management dynamic. Try this one on:

To me there is no difference between a manager and a coach. As a manager, you are responsible for the performance of your team – your direct reports. Your objective is not to win a game, but it is to manage your team's efforts to accomplish your mission. If there is no clearly defined mission, that is a problem and we need to fix that by clearly stating it, understanding it, and communicating it. But that's another chapter. Let's assume we have and understand the mission. Now it's time for leadership. Whether you're the manager or the coach, you must assess your team's strengths and weaknesses. You must evaluate the skills that will be needed to accomplish the mission (or win games), and determine if your team possesses those skills. If not, you need to determine if the missing skills and talents can be taught to the existing team, or if you will need to recruit new team members. In real life, just as on the sports teams, there is sometimes a limit on the number of players that can be on a team. It makes no financial sense at all to pay extra people to sit on the bench if they aren't capable of contributing to the team's success. At some point you will have to decide if you are happy with your team making small and incremental movement in the direction of the mission (winning a game or two each year), or if you want to have a championship team. This analogy could go on forever, but I think you probably get the main points by now. Even though, when you were in elementary school you were the best player on the court, you found that the competition in high school to make the team was much greater. And even though you may have been a man among boys in high school, trying to make a college team made you feel like a beginner. And imagine what a professional athlete that plays for a championship caliber team has to do to keep his spot in the starting lineup.

You are a professional operations manager. Does your team fully understand the mission? Have you assessed their strengths and weaknesses? Have you trained, led, and coached your team? Have you managed them in a way that allows them to use their strengths while recognizing the need to get support in their weaker areas, and pitch in to fill the gaps created by other team member's weaknesses? Is your team one that wins a game or two, or are they determined to have a championship team?

In today's market, good managers are very hard to find. Most of them that are really good are being very well taken care of, and are happy where they are. Today's managers must become cultivators of their own talent. Keep your eyes open for potential in the people that already work in your organization. Talk to them about their longer term careers. Help them to get the training and experiences that they will need in their future steps in their career development. Mentor and coach them. Help them to become the future talent pool for your company. Help them to earn their jersey.

Don't be the coach that is just trying to get through the season without getting fired. Be the coach that builds a championship caliber team.

As I look back over my career it is interesting what you remember. It's not the productivity records that you set, or the awards that you won, or even the recognition received from your customers. What makes me feel good about the time I spent in operations is all of the people that started as part of my team and grew into other roles where they became leaders and coaches of "championship" teams, and to think that in some small way, I may have helped them to get there.

There is another point that needs to be made when talking about success in your chosen profession. The point is best illustrated with an actual "lesson learned" that happened early in my operational management career. At the time, I was the manager of a production area, and reported to the facility general manager. Let's call him Barry. I had an issue that I needed to discuss with Barry. As I knocked on his open door, I could see that he was at his desk, and looking out of his window into the parking lot. My knock on the door startled him a bit, and as he tuned to look my way, I noticed that his eyes were a little red and he clearly been shedding a tear or two. Trying not to appear too nosey, I just asked if everything was OK. He looked at me with a seriousness that was rare for him. He said, "Terry, you are very young. Take some advice from an old guy. Don't let what has happened to me, happen to you". I asked what had happened. He said, "My wife just called to tell me that my youngest daughter had gotten engaged to be married. I know I should be happy about it. She's marrying a great guy. But it's made me realize that I really don't know her very well. She was born when I was a young, eager, up and coming manager like you, and I spent way too much time trying to get the next promotion. When she was starting school, I had just relocated to a new city for a new promotion. My wife took care of getting the kids in school, doctor's appointments, parent teacher conferences, and practically everything else that needed to be done. I went to work, and spent long days on the job, not to mention all of the meetings and dinners and travel that was business related. That scenario repeated itself several more times as I took promotions and relocated to new plants. Even when I was home, I was thinking about work issues. The kids grew up, went off to college, started careers and families of their own, and I went to work. And as I sit here today thinking about my little girl that's about to be married, I am asking myself if it was worth it, and there's no question that it was not. My advice to you, Terry, is to make sure you find the right balance between your work life and your personal life. Everyone is different in their priorities and their drive to succeed in all aspects of life. Spend a little time evaluating your priorities and what's important to you, and make sure that when you're an old guy like me, that you won't be sorry for the choices you've made."

I never forgot Barry's advice. There were times when either I realized, or someone close to me reminded me, that I was letting my work consume me, and I needed to adjust those priorities. As I sit here, about the age Barry was when he shared his thoughts, I'm pretty satisfied with the choices I've made in prioritization of my time. Of course, there were things I would change if I could, but I will always be thankful that my boss took the time, and cared enough to share his thoughts and feelings with me that day. It absolutely made a difference in the choices that I made.

7. Don't crush creativity by telling everyone what to do step by step, but……

Back in chapter 4, I talked about the fundamentals of manufacturing. This chapter is an attempt to expound and clarify that idea.

One of my former bosses, let's call him Bobby, was another case study in learning valuable lessons by teaching you what NOT to do. In less than two years, he single handedly ruined the performance of more than 30 supervisors and mid-level managers. While doing so, the plant had excellent results. How can that be?

Bobby was a very smart guy, with tons of manufacturing experience and endless energy. If you were looking for someone to come into a poor performing plant and turn it around, he was your guy. From his first month on the job, all performance indicators started to improve. From an upper management point of view, he was the best manager in the company. He was told many times that he was the best, and to keep up the good work. He was not only rewarded with praise, he was also promoted and received several monetary rewards for the great performance turnaround he was achieving. It wasn't until he was promoted to another facility that some of the upper management started to realize the mistake they had made. For those of us at the plant, it seemed obvious, but an atmosphere had been created where to say anything negative to upper management regarding their "Golden Boy" would be like talking bad about motherhood and apple pie. If anything that even resembled criticism was uttered, the immediate response would be something like, "have you seen the performance numbers?????"

The fact was that Bobby was the best manager of processes, systems, machines, and logistics that I have worked with, but also among the worst managers of people I had ever seen. He would personally implement systems and new processes, and make changes to equipment and standards, but never once tell anyone "WHY" he was doing what he was doing. I never heard him ask his subordinates a question like, what do you think, or how do you suggest we address this issue? He simply told everyone what to do, how to do it, and when it had to be done. If you asked any questions, the response was usually, "I don't have time to explain it right now, just get it done and we'll talk about it later".

When he moved on to his next assignment, performance plummeted. The poor interim manager tried to maintain things, but he was no match for the knowledge and experience, not to mention the endless energy of Bobby. Most of the supervisors had been reprogrammed to believe that they were no longer supposed to think, use initiative, or take any sort of action, unless of course someone told them what to do, how to do it, and when to have it done. Some knew they should go back to doing their jobs the way they used to do them, but frankly, they didn't want to. The job is a whole lot easier if I just coast until someone tells me to do something.

It has taken years to get managers to recover from Bobby's style of leadership. Some would tell you that there are still some supervisors that have done their best to hang onto the idea that I don't have to do anything until I'm specifically told to do it. It is great to have the knowledge and experience that Bobby had. And yes, it may have taken a little longer, but think of the success he could have created if he saw the objective differently. If he saw the objective as a teacher. A coach and teacher that was going to transfer what he knew to others. To make each of his subordinates a better manager because they had learned from him. Think of the added value that would have brought to this company, if he developed 5 or 10 or 20 people to be able to teach others these skills and abilities.

Maybe the biggest loss in Bobby's management style is how much HE may have learned and added to his own overall performance, had he taken the time and effort to talk and teach and coach and work with the people he came in contact with, rather than just telling them what to do, how to do it, and when to have it done.

It was a Chinese philosopher that said it best: Give a man a fish and you feed him for a day. Teach a man to fish and you feed him for a lifetime.

As I write this, I am working with a new manager in a very large plant that has severe performance problems. The new manager has done an excellent job of creating the mission – where we are going and how we are going to get there. He and his team have implemented new production systems, tools, procedures, and routines. Performance of the plant has improved significantly in a short period of time. However, much of the change in results can be attributed to the new manager's individual effort. He has brought his direct reports along, but he has clearly been the driver of all of the changes, and a very "hands on" part of everything that has been done. If he were to leave today, there is little doubt in my mind that the poor results would return even faster than they appeared. Why?

He is now in a phase where he must transfer ownership of the mission to others. It's now all about changing the goals and objectives of the people that work for him, and the people that work for them. They need to be recognized and rewarded for implementing their own processes, training their people, and teaching others about what we are doing and why. They need to move from the thought process of "pleasing the boss by doing what he wants", to one of "developing procedures and processes that insure the mission is achieved". It's no longer "what the boss wants", its "how do we insure mission success". You don't win games by watching the scoreboard. You win games by executing the fundamentals perfectly every time, and if you do that, the scoreboard takes care of itself. This is now the key objective of the manager, to gradually replace his constant driving presence in the shop by teaching and coaching others to take over and eventually make this an atmosphere of continual improvement standard operating procedure.

I don't mean to make this process sound easy, it is not. First of all, everyone develops an understanding and makes progress at a different pace. So, one type and style of teaching and coaching does not work with everyone. Some will take longer to "get it" than others, and some may never "get it" and will need to be replaced. Some days you will feel that you are going backwards, and progress has slipped. It happens, so don't be discouraged.

When my kids were small, I helped coach a beginners "T-Ball" league. There were kids that had older siblings they played with, and were actually pretty good ball players. There were others who had never held a bat or threw a baseball. They all learned the fundamentals at a different pace. I needed to spend a lot more coaching time with some than with others. Yes, some tried my patience more than others as well. But, by the first game, they all were able to participate, and they all improved as the season progressed. There were a few of the really bad beginners that ended up being some of our best players.

8. Have and communicate a clear mission/direction that is not negotiable

After working with hundreds of manufacturing plants, and seeing everything from unbelievably outstanding performance, to performance so bad the plant was destined for failure….. There is one thing I can say for certain that all of the best plants have had in common: A crystal clear vision/direction of where the plant was going, and how it was going to get there.

Please do not misinterpret the above to mean that you need to spend days with your team at an offsite meeting, coming up with some eloquent and all-encompassing vision statement to put on a plaque in your front lobby. As a matter of fact, the simpler the better on this one, please. It should be something that truly reflects where you plan to take the business, and how you plan to get there. Everyone in the organization needs to be able to not only understand it, but be able to support it and help make it happen.

Imagine yourself as an operator of a machine in the factory. The CEO of the company comes to the plant for an all employee meeting to unveil the mission of the company. After the ceremony and obligatory speeches and fanfare, it is presented:

"It is our mission to continue to authoritatively provide access to diverse products and services to insure we stay relevant in tomorrow's world."

Now that you understand the mission/vision, what will you do differently in your job to assist the company in accomplishing the mission? If you have a good answer to that question, please let me know what it is because I have no idea how I could translate that statement into action at any level of the organization. It is however, a real mission statement from a real company.

One company that I worked with literally took months trying to perfect their mission statement. Why? Because they were spending their time trying to find the perfect words to communicate to their employees, stockholders, customers, suppliers, managers, neighbors, community, and everyone else they could think of, without offending any of them. That is the main reason a lot of companies have mission statements that make no sense. The mission statement is not something you should use to try to impress anyone. It is also not intended to get any response or results from anyone other than your employees. If you want to impress your stockholders, customers, suppliers, managers, neighbors, community, and everyone else you can think of, come up with a slogan or tag line, and hang that in your lobby, on your brochures, on the outside of your building, or on your advertising. Again, the mission statement is for your employees – so they know where you want to take the business – so they can help you get there.

Also, the mission statement is not necessarily a permanent fixture, cast in stone. It should be looked at as something that can be modified, or changed completely at some point in the future. For example, I might have a mission statement for my business that goes something like this:

"Our mission is to reverse the current trend of red ink, and return the company to financial stability, through improving operating efficiency, reducing our costs, and achieving customer service levels that are clearly the best in our industry".

Reading this, I think every employee in the organization could generate some ideas around how they personally could do some things to help accomplish this mission. However, at some point in the future, if we are successful, and we achieve sustained financial stability, we may need to modify this statement.

Some will look at this and say – Where is safety in your mission statement? Some will say – What about employee involvement? Some may say – Where is community involvement? Some may say – What about treating your suppliers as partners? Not including these or other things is not a statement saying those things aren't important. Of course they are important. But when you add in everything that is important, you confuse your employees. When you ask them for everything, then you are asking them to sort out where the priorities lie, and for those that are looking for one, you have provided an excuse for them to focus on none of them. Keep your mission simple, easy to understand, and most importantly, easy to find ways to support.

I once did some work for a man that owned his own business. He was a very religious man, and wanted everyone one to know that, in his life, and therefore also in his business, God was the CEO, and His Word, The Bible, would be the employee handbook. His mission statement was made up of several references from the Bible, regarding how to treat others, expectations of workers and bosses, etc. His business failed, not in any small part due to some of his workers who, let's just say didn't have the same level of respect for God's Word.

Some of my very good friends and I disagree on this point, and after many discussions, we can agree to disagree. I do not believe that a specific religion has a place in the workplace. Nor do I believe that a specific political party has a place in the workplace. There could certainly be exceptions to this, particularly in smaller businesses where it could be feasible that all of the employees and managers were all of the same religious and/or political beliefs. But in larger organizations, my advice is to make the workplace neutral ground for both religion and politics. I have seen many examples where these two issues have taken the focus away from the work that people are being paid to do. I have seen hard feelings develop between workers that were once happy to work together, because of allowing their personal beliefs to be advertised within the workplace. I'm pretty certain that the ACLU might take exception with some of my views, but my stance was and continues to be – practice your religion and your politics on your own time to your heart's content. But, check your beliefs on those subjects at the door, before you come to work. Please understand that I in no way mean to be disrespectful towards any religion. I consider myself a Christian. I personally would have no issue with a group of Christians using the conference room for a Bible study meeting once a week before the start of their shift. But when my co-worker wants to use the conference room once a week for a meeting of the American Nazi Party of which he and a few others are members, is that OK? Members of The Church of Modern Witchcraft? Where does it end? What does it have to do with the "MISSION"?

I obviously understand that you will never keep all of these influences out of your businesses. However, it is up to you as managers to make sure you are getting your people focused on doing the work they are being paid to do, and to keep, as much as possible, a cooperative attitude and some degree of harmony among your workforce. So the first time a Democrat comes in wearing a derogatory T-shirt with a picture that could be offensive to a Republican, or the reverse happens, try to stop it in its tracks. Otherwise, you will have the opposite side's derogatory T-shirt worn the next day by someone to retaliate. And this type of thing can escalate to an all-out war. I have been in some plants where local sports team rivalries are so intense, that they are just as bad as religion or politics! The bottom line is that they are being paid to stay focused on a specific job, and that job should not include politics, religion, or any other extracurricular activity that takes you away from the mission.

Once you have come to the point that the mission is clearly defined and communicated, the mission is NON-NEGOTIABLE. What exactly does that mean? It means that members of the management team must give that mission 100% of their support. If, for whatever reason, they feel they cannot support the mission at that level, they must be removed from the management team immediately and possibly from the entire company. It is extremely important that the entire salaried workforce supports the mission.

I have witnessed many managers over the years that were highly educated and extremely intelligent, but were total failures at their jobs simply because they were cowards when it comes to giving straight and clear performance feedback to their subordinates. They didn't want to be seen as the "bad guy", or they didn't want to "make someone mad at them". Sometimes it was because there were family relationships involved, so the hard feelings were taken home to others that were related. When your employee is not performing their job the way you want them to, and you chose to turn your head to it, who do you think benefits from your non-action? The subordinate? Your customers? You? Your company? The answer is no one benefits. It is simply you choosing to abdicate the responsibilities you were hired to perform, and everyone loses as a result. The subordinate may not even realize that he is performing below your expectations, and consequently will never have an opportunity to improve what he is unaware of. And remember, this feedback is not to be punitive; it is intended to identify an opportunity to help the employee improve so the team is more successful and moving closer to accomplishing the mission.

There is some controversy over who actually coined the phrase, but whether it was Thomas Paine or someone else, they were right on when they said, "Lead, Follow, or Get Out Of The Way". Managers are hired and put into their roles to lead. If you are a manager that is not capable of giving your subordinates clear direction, clear guidance on your expectations, and the training and tools to enable success, and then you fail to give them feedback and hold them accountable for meeting your expectations of them, you need to get into one of the other two categories – become a follower or get out of the way.

Please understand that I am not suggesting every manager should become some sort of autocratic tyrant. It should be understood that all of your actions must be professional and compassionate with the goal being performance improvement. But if you choose to turn your head to less than desirable performance, in the name of being a more enlightened manager, you are making excuses for your own poor performance.

The fact is that performance evaluation and feedback is an extremely important part of a manager's responsibility. After all, your subordinate's performance, collectively, and ultimately, is a reflection of your performance. It is also a very subjective and emotional process. Many attempts have been made to make the process more objective and less emotional, but in my opinion, some of those efforts have gone too far in that direction. I have seen some "performance appraisal systems" that essentially give the manager an excuse to do a poor job evaluating performance and giving feedback. "I have to use this scale and those are the only numbers it provides". "I don't really believe your performance is that bad, but that's what the numbers add up to". "There are other aspects of your performance I'd like to consider, but this is the form we have to use".

I once had a supervisor that worked for me that taught me a couple valuable lessons about performance appraisals. He would come to my office at least once a month, and ask how he was doing. At first I would say things like, "you haven't been here very long, but so far you're doing fine". But, after a couple of those, he said, "That type of feedback isn't helping me. I want to know what you think I can do better". As I began to highlight some areas where I thought he could improve, he would smile and thank me for the feedback. He really thrived on it. Once, after giving him some feedback on something I felt he could stand to improve, I asked him if he agreed with my assessment. He said, "No, but that really doesn't matter, does it"? When I asked what he meant by that, he said, "It's all about perception isn't it? My perception is that I'm doing fine in that area. But you perceive that I need to improve. So whether I need to change the performance depends on the results we get. But for sure, I need to change your perception". That young supervisor is today the CEO of a large corporation.

9. The Balanced Scorecard

As I look back over the hundreds of manufacturing operations that I have toured in my career, and select the best and the worst five plants, both groups have several things in common. Many of those common characteristics are discussed on these pages. One very consistent trait that the five best share that I have not talked a lot about is plant performance measurements.

Once you have established a crystal clear vision, or mission – you know where you want to go and how you will get there – how will you know on a daily, weekly, monthly, quarterly basis if you are making progress in the right direction? How will you measure success or failure in those intervals? Please take the time to think this through before throwing out the normal answers like, "safety is our number one priority", or "quality comes first – we never compromise quality". How you determine your performance measurements demands some serious thought, because if you are not careful, you could be your own worst enemy. Read on.

First line supervisors in all organizations, and a couple organizational levels up in most operations, will take what you establish as the metrics as the main source for how their performance will be judged – and for the most part, that is a good assumption. It is my experience as a supervisor, and from working with hundreds of them over the years, that supervisors rarely do anything intentionally sinister to make themselves look good at the expense of the company. However, having said that, supervisors will, and do put a focus and a priority on what they have been told are the measurements of their performance. So, be careful what you ask for.

First of all, never prioritize one performance metric over the rest. Terry, why was your delivery performance so poor yesterday? Reply: You told me that safety was our highest priority, and that nothing was to come before an absolute dedication to making sure our employees were safe at all times. So, I shut the line down for a half day to discuss safety and brainstorm with the employees on how we can insure we are working safely. You don't want me to put delivery performance ahead of safety, do you???????

While that may be an extreme example, that metric that you have raised above all others can quickly and easily become the scapegoat for poor performance in other areas.

Secondly, keep the list of metrics short – the fewer the better. I believe that every business is unique, and based on the vision of where you are taking the business; you may have different measurements of success, and therefore different metrics. Hence, it would be foolish for me to tell you what the metrics should be, but whatever they are, try to limit them to no more than five (5). I would like every employee to know and clearly understand all of the measurements, and give them all an equal focus, and that is difficult to do if there are 18 of them.

One of the biggest frustrations of first line supervisors is changing metrics. I am absolutely convinced that some of my prior bosses had this method of determining what metric was the most important: I believe they studied the results carefully, and found the one metric where we had performed poorly, and that was the most important. Delivery was the most important when it was bad, but as soon as that improved it wasn't that important anymore, and the focus moved to my poor quality. Until that improved, then it was inventory that stunk. Etc., etc., etc..

Think through your choices of metric before publishing them.

When I was a young supervisor, we had a long list of metrics that we were told would be used as the basis of our performance appraisals. However, everyone knew that the only one that REALLY mattered was labor efficiency. So, most of our efforts were aimed at having a high labor efficiency number. There were lots of ways to improve the number. The most obvious was to make more parts with less labor. But that was also the one that required the most effort. You could also make sure you ran the parts that had the easiest standards or the ones that ran the best. Of course, those may not have any customer orders due while the other parts that we avoided did. Not good for delivery performance, or for inventory turns, but made the labor efficiency look great. Then there was always the never work on indirect labor trick. So you would avoid any rework, maintenance activities, or clean up, and try to leave that to another crew or another shift. None of which is in the best interest of the plant or the customer.

I recently worked with a plant where the SVP of Ops made it well know that he thought OAE was the most important measure of performance of a plant. So guess what? The main driver in all of his plants was to have a high OAE number. OAE is a measure of how well a facility is utilizing its capital asset base, and may be a good indicator for someone in his position to use when making capital purchase decisions. However, because it has become "the" measure in this company, they make some absolutely stupid decisions about running machines and making inventory and using labor in the name of running a good OAE number. Again, decisions that are not in the best interest of the plant or the customer.

Another great example of measurements gone rouge is purchasing. I have been witness to two different companies performing this SNAFU. The main goal of all purchasing agents in the company is to get all of our vendors to 90 day terms. The suppliers aren't stupid. They understand the time value of money as well. So what do they do? Accept the payment terms at 90 days, but at the same time raise their prices – some by as much as 30%!!!!!! The purchasing agent doesn't care so much about the price because they aren't being measured on the price. They are, however being measured on their average payment term days!!!! Again, not in the company's best interest.

Carefully select the metrics that will clearly indicate the performance factors that are important to your business objectives. Keep the number down to five or less, and keep them consistent so people can clearly understand what they will be measured on. Make sure it is clear that they are all important, and doing well on one is not an excuse to do poorly on another. It is not an either/or proposition.

Just as an aside…. This week, I learned that a company that I had previously worked with, now under new leadership, had announced this year's metrics for their management incentive program (bonus scheme). It was to be based on just two measurements: EBITDA and Cash Flow. In my humble opinion, this will be a long term strategic blunder. They have just communicated that the only important metrics are those two. I predict there will be very bad decisions made that will jeopardize customer service, quality, safety, employee relations, and many other aspects of the business in the name of financial performance. Of course no one will admit openly that they are putting less effort into these other areas, but the two that pay will get the highest priority every time.

10. What you do doesn't matter as much as how you do it

Over the years of studying hundreds of manufacturing operations, I have asked myself this question over and over: Is it what they do that makes them successful, or is it how they do it? Let me explain:

My first experience in transforming a plant from underperforming to over achieving is at the heart of many of the lessons learned in this writing. As has been previously described, we fundamentally changed the way the plant was managed, and the way we had all learned to do our jobs. We also changed the flow of product from a very "functional" organization with departments of like processes, to a "product line" organization with connected processes of like products. As the years went by, I have often wondered if we would have been as successful if we had stayed with the old product flow organization. After seeing "Common Sense Manufacturing" implemented in many different types of manufacturing environments, I have come to the conclusion that absolutely we would have been just as successful.

The reason is because it wasn't what we did that made us successful, it was because of how we did it. First, the implementation of "Common Sense Manufacturing" was our "MISSION". It was led from the very top of the organization, and moved downward through and to the lowest levels. It was not optional. As managers and supervisors, you either supported it with 100% of your efforts, or you began searching for your next career opportunity. The training and the rules by which the shop floor production systems were operated were straight forward, easily understood by all, and followed. Failure to follow the rules of the systems was met with immediate and stern warnings, and repeated violations could (and did) result in termination of employment. Small initial improvement was recognized, and quickly grew into widespread improvements and a feeling of accomplishment throughout the organization. There began to be a friendly competition between the various product lines to see who could be more aggressive with their production systems, and achieve better results.

Because of the above, I have decided that it really doesn't matter that much "WHAT" you do. But if you make it optional, it will fail. If you and the entire organization are not giving it their full support, it will fail. If there is not a strict adherence to the rules and policies that govern the systems, it will fail.

I have worked with organizations that, in my opinion are some of the best manufacturers in the world. I have also worked with organizations that are at the opposite end of that spectrum. And, I have worked with many that are in between. I have become a firm believer that where you sit on that spectrum is directly proportionate to how closely you come to adhering to the previous couple of paragraphs. When what you do stops being what you do, and becomes who you are, it is almost impossible to not be successful.

I know of a company that makes it known that "their thing" is "Six Sigma". If you look at any article or literature on the company, Six Sigma is all over it. If you hire in as an employee at any level, a large part of your orientation is about their signature operational fundamentals of the use of Six Sigma. Six Sigma, simply defined is a data driven methodology to eliminate defects. But to this company, it is way more than that. It is who they are. If you work there, you understand it, and it is part of your job every day. It is not an option for you to decide to take on a different philosophy for managing your part of the operation. And by the way, this company is very successful. But wait – many companies claim to use Six Sigma Methodology, but aren't very successful. That's because IT'S NOT ABOUT WHAT THEY DO – IT'S ABOUT HOW THEY DO IT.

I have sat in countless conference rooms and listened to presentation after presentation of how the operation has used SMED, JIT Manufacturing, Kan Ban, Kaizen, TPM, 5S, and twenty other "tools". And in those same organizations, when I went to the shop floor, I would see almost none of what they had talked about in the conference room. What I did see was usually a superficial implementation with displays and charts that either were not being used, were out of date, contained inaccurate information, or all of the above. Too often the reason for this was because someone higher up had mentioned that they believed OAE is the best measure of productivity, or the CEO likes Six Sigma, or the Operations Director is a fan of TPM. They treat these tools like they are in a supermarket and picking up a couple of those and a few of these. Then they are surprised when they go to the shop floor and see that they have been superficially implemented and there is no discipline for following the procedures and rules.

There are literally hundreds of useful tools that can be used in manufacturing operations to assist with improving performance. But you first have to decide who or what you want to be when you grow up. Create and communicate where you are going and how you are going to get there. Make that become who you are, not what you do. Provide the leadership to take your workforce on that journey with you. Let it be known to all that everyone needs to be in the same boat and rowing in the same direction. Reinforce that with immediate course correction when they start to stray. Celebrate the successes, and the failures, and reward those that take measured risks in the furtherance of the mission.

How these implementations are structured into the organization is another key to success or failure. They MUST be driven from the top of the organization, and each layer below MUST have accountability for the implementation for their areas of responsibility. You are only kidding yourself if you think you can hire a "Lean Implementation Expert" to install Lean techniques in your operation, and have him/her report to someone that reports to someone that reports to someone. I have known many very frustrated "Continual Improvement Coordinators" that have tried to get operations people to get involved and support what they were trying to do, only to have operations supervisors and managers give them little or no support. And then, of course, the poor continual improvement coordinator was seen as ineffective because he/she failed to get the processes and systems implemented. On the other hand, if the operations guys are the ones held accountable for the implementation, and they use the continual improvement coordinator as a resource to assist them in THEIR implementation, there is a much higher opportunity for successful implementations. If the top one or two people in your organization are not committed to whatever it is you are trying to accomplish, and will not hold the people that report to them accountable for the success of the initiative, you can expect the level of success to be equal to the level of their commitment.

11. When you "get it", it's no longer what we do, it's who we are

If there is one thing I have learned over the years, it's that while everyone is different, most people in manufacturing plants are very similar. I have worked in manufacturing plants all over the world and it is amazing to me how alike people are. Whether it is Mexico, Europe, China, or the U.S., people tend to react to change in the exact same way. What impacts how people react is not the people, but the situation that they find themselves in. If you want me to help you improve your operation, first, you must want my help. As an operations consultant (both internally to the company I worked for, and as a self-employed consultant) I have experienced several futile attempts at operational improvement, simply because upper management really didn't have a deep desire to improve. Seems kind of crazy, doesn't it? They really didn't want to improve??????? Actually, they do want to improve, so long as THEY don't have to change. So long as it's not really disruptive to our normal routine. So long as we don't upset anyone. So long as it doesn't require any changes in people, positions, or responsibilities. And the list goes on. Remember the definition of insanity? Continuing the same actions, and expecting a different result. A lot of people want the results to change, but they are not willing to do the work, make the changes, and get out of their comfort zones long enough to actually allow improvement to take place.

I could give many real life examples that would illustrate what I am talking about, but here is the first that comes to mind:

I was asked to assist a company in changing their family owned business from a company where the owner worked 24/7 and made virtually every decision required, to a team atmosphere so a manager and a management team split up the responsibility and shared the management of the company. I spent a half of a day with the owner, trying to get the answer to one question – Are you willing and ready to make this change? She insisted that she was ready, however several things that she said during our conversation told me that she was not going to be comfortable "letting go" of some of her responsibility and authority. I was crystal clear with her that if she couldn't let go of that authority, and pass it on to a management team, that the initiative would be doomed for failure. She insisted that she didn't have a choice. That she wanted to eventually retire, and didn't want others to become the same workaholic that she had become. So we gave it a try. For several months, things went pretty well. She actually started to let go of some of his responsibility and authority. I introduced them to job descriptions, and business planning, and work rules and policy manuals, so there would be some structure to the organization. We spent a few days defining a mission for the company, and some firm direction of where we wanted to go and how we planned to get there. We developed an organization chart that included a management team and all of their direct reports, with no names in the boxes. When that was completed, I asked her to closely examine the job descriptions that we had developed, complete with qualifications, experience, and education level for each position on the management team. Then I asked her to determine if we had current employees that – based on the job descriptions – would be excellent candidates to fill those positions, or if we would need to go outside to get the talent and experience that we had determined was needed. A few days later at our next meeting, she had a name in every box for the management team – all of which were members of her family. In most cases it was clear that they were not even close to meeting the requirements. We started to have a discussion about it, but it quickly became clear that she didn't intend to allow anyone other than a family member on the management team. It was just as clear that there was nothing I could do to help her, if she wasn't willing to make some changes and release some of her tight grip of control. Why? Because she really didn't want any help. She was willing to put a management team in place, but in name only. She still wanted complete control.

Whether you are talking about a 5S implementation or a SMED activity, or a Kaizen Event, or just about any other system implementation or change, the hardest part of being successful is sustaining what you have implemented. I have witnessed some remarkable improvements, only to see them fade away over time because the organization was not able to sustain what they had done.

It is hard, and I am in no way suggesting that it requires anything but extreme dedication to make it work. But, the only thing that will allow your improvements to be sustained is discipline, discipline, and discipline. There must be constant follow-up to insure policies, procedures, and rules are adhered to without exception. Violations must be dealt with swiftly and aggressively. People that repeatedly violate the systems must be retrained, and if the issues cannot be resolved, they may need to be removed. Everyone doesn't necessarily need to be a disciple, but managers and supervisors must give the systems 100% support, and cannot turn their heads to violations. If they are not willing to give that level of commitment, they cannot be managers and supervisors in this organization.

When you get to that level of commitment, your systems are no longer what you do, they become who you are. Once they become who you are, every new employee comes into the organization learning this is who you will have to become if you want to work here, and you will reach a point where the constant follow up can cease because there is no other way that is even considered.

12. Bobby Knight – "Your players will be satisfied with the level of performance you are satisfied with"

I once listened to a speech by former Indiana University basketball coach, Bobby Knight. To be clear, I was never a huge fan of Mr. Knight, but he said something in this speech that I found to be a very true statement, and one that all managers should spend some time thinking about.

In earlier chapters, I told you about two supervisors that I had in my early working career, Rich and Willy.

Willy had very low expectations of his subordinates and even lower expectations of himself. He spent very little time talking to or observing the performance of his employees. Everyone knew this and just assumed (correctly) that he just didn't care how they performed, so long as it wasn't bad enough to get his boss's attention in which case he would have to actually come out of hiding to actually try to find out what the problem was. Most employees knew exactly what they needed to do to keep their performance slightly above the minimum level. I remember thinking that some of them are working harder at finding ways to goof off than they would if they just did their job.

While he was always professional and courteous, Rich always had an expectation of my performance that was just a little bit higher than I was currently performing. Not just me, but of all of his direct reports. Just when I thought I had satisfied everything he was expecting of me, he raised the bar just a little higher. He continually challenged me to do just a little more, to go just a little further, to reach just a little higher. He didn't raise the bar so high that I would give up, but just a little bit higher than where I happened to be. Yes, it became a game for me to try to get ahead of his expectations, although I don't think I ever did. Or maybe I did. I just knew that I never wanted to disappoint him by falling short of the level of his confidence in me.

Mr. Knight's words really hit a chord with me. He was so right. Whether it is your boss, your coach, your parents, or just someone that you have respect for, their expectations of you really do have an impact on the level of performance that you become satisfied with. This chapter is dedicated to Rich, who taught me a valuable lesson in management of people. And, he did it by the example that he displayed to us every day by simply doing his job the best way he could. He was not an educated man. He worked his way up through the chain and eventually became a third shift supervisor, and one of the best managers of people I ever had the pleasure of working with. I know a lot of high level managers, directors, VP's, and even a couple CEO's that could learn a great deal from his example.

Summary

So, based on a lifetime of experience, and visiting hundreds of plants I have come to the conclusion that every truly outstanding manufacturing operation – and I've seen several – have five very specific things in common. They are listed below. I would invite you to carefully and objectively analyze your own organization with respect to each of the following keys. After being completely honest with yourself while doing this analysis, do these keys exist in your organization? Where the answer is no, is it possible to get them in place? How would you go about doing that?

Purpose – Where are you going and how are you going to get there? Is there a clear and concise "Mission Statement"? The "Mission" or "Vision" of the enterprise must be understood to be supported. It must be understood by the organization, and management must embrace it with passion. Every decision the business takes must be supported by management, and the work force must see and believe that it is real. All decisions and initiatives must support the mission. The entire organization must support it, or find another place to work.

People - Do you have the right organization to fit your mission, and do you have the right people in each of the key organizational slots (job descriptions, the right experience and knowledge, diversity of input, clearly defined mission, goals and objectives, standard work, regular and effective performance feedback, accountability for performance, rewards for top performers, and consequences for non-performance)?

Process – Are the fundamentals of manufacturing defined? Does the workforce understand the mission, and does the production system allow them to be involved in running the shop? Does the workforce understand why they are making what they are making when they are making it? Does the production system provide an incentive for continual improvement? Is discipline on the shop floor respected and enforced?

Profitability – Does the business case make financial sense? Are there accurate methods and systems to understand material cost? Labor cost? Overhead cost? Is there an adequate process for quoting new business? Is there a process in place to regularly review pricing and profitability by part number, and is there a process to deal with losing businesses?

Passion – True operational success doesn't happen without passion. You have to care. It can't just be a job or a way to make a living. It also can't be artificial. Leadership must show by their actions that there are certain things that are very important, and those things will get attention and priority. The rest of the organization will clearly see from this leadership, and as a result, will be able support and make progress towards the purpose. Do your managers and leaders display a passion for the business, or do some appear to be just "doing their job"?

Think of the rules, policies, and procedures of your production system as the building blocks of a solid impenetrable stone wall that will protect the organization from failure of the manufacturing operations. You can maintain the strength of this wall with an unwavering and steadfast dedication to the mission, and to the rules, policies, and procedures that support that mission. Every time you allow a rule to be ignored or not completely followed, you loosen some mortar between the stones. Every time you turn your head to the violation of a policy, more mortar falls by the wayside. Every time you choose to "bend" the rules, another stone becomes loose. When those of you at the top positions of manufacturing make decisions that others perceive to be allowing anything less than a fanatical adherence to the mission, you have given your permission for further violations of the systems. Before you realize it, your impenetrable wall has become a loose pile of rubble that protects you from nothing.

I have seen so many companies that try to emulate great manufacturing operations by duplicating the production systems and tools that they use. But they are completely missing the key to their success. When I first sat down to start this book, my intention was to explain how to accomplish continual improvement of operational excellence in manufacturing. It wasn't until I had almost finished that I fully realized that there is very little here regarding the mechanics of the systems used in Lean Manufacturing. It is all about people, relationships, communication, interpersonal relations, and working together towards an objective. It's not about the system or the tool. It is about creating a culture of total adherence and support of the mission, and the systems and the tools are just that: tools to aid in that effort. I guess Greg was right; we are in the people business.

One of the most copied manufacturing companies in the word is Toyota. The Toyota manager credited with being "The Father of the Toyota Production System" summed it up this way:

"The key to the Toyota Way and what makes Toyota stand out is not any of the individual elements...But what is important is having all the elements together as a system. It must be practiced every day in a very consistent

manner, not in spurts."
-- Taiichi Ohno

At the beginning of this writing, I mentioned that the plant I was running at the time of my retirement was at peak performance. Less than two years later, there has been enough change in personnel, ideas, priorities, and deterioration in the adherence to the disciplines of the production systems, that the performance has again slipped to an unacceptable level. Productivity, Quality, Customer Service, and Profitability have all deteriorated. While very disappointing, it just reinforces what I have said several times, and in several ways in the above pages. Those "5 P's" a few pages back ALL MUST BE PRESENT. Almost all manufacturing organizations are good, maybe excellent, at one or two, or even three of them. Very few can check all five boxes. If they can, I'm buying their stock because they will be a huge success!

"If you always do what you've always done you will always get what you always got."

Henry Ford

Printed in Great Britain
by Amazon